Searchlight BOOKS

The World of Gaming

The World of

Pokémon

Buffy Silverman

Lerner Publications ◆ Minneapolis

To Emma, my favorite Pokémon trainer

Lerner Publications Company
A division of Lerner Publishing Group, Inc.
241 First Avenue North
Minneapolis, MN 55401 USA

For reading levels and more information, look up this title
at www.lernerbooks.com.

Library of Congress Cataloging-in-Publication Data

The Cataloging-in-Publication Data for *The World of Pokémon* is on file at the Library of
    Congress.
ISBN 978-1-5124-8310-9 (lib. bdg.)
ISBN 978-1-5415-1199-6 (pbk.)
ISBN 978-1-5124-8314-7 (EB pdf)

Manufactured in the United States of America
1-43327-33147-8/22/2017

Contents

Chapter 1

POKÉMON: THE EARLY DAYS

You're walking on the beach when the phone in your hand vibrates. The screen shows a Psyduck waving its arms near the water. You aim, throw a Poké Ball, and the Psyduck is yours!

People of all ages enjoy catching Pokémon.

People have been catching and trading Pokémon for more than twenty years. Pokémon appear in video games, card games, and lots of other places. They may look like unusual birds or cats. Some resemble dragons or dinosaurs. There's almost no end to the variety of Pokémon creatures.

People who play Pokémon are called trainers. As a trainer, your goal is to catch Pokémon. Then you train them by using them in battles so they level up and grow strong.

Fans played the original Pokémon games on a handheld device called a Game Boy. Nintendo released these games, called *Pokémon Red* and *Pokémon Green*, in Japan in 1996. Together, the games introduced 151 Pokémon.

Neither version of the game actually had 151 Pokémon. To catch them all, a trainer with *Pokémon Red* had to trade with someone who had *Pokémon Green*. A Game Boy cable let players link their devices and trade Pokémon. Trainers could also enter their Pokémon into battles with each other.

These trainers had a blast trading Pokémon on their Game Boys!

Meet Satoshi Tajiri

What inspired Pokémon inventor Satoshi Tajiri to create the popular critters? When he was a boy, he loved catching insects. His friends called him Dr. Bug. This interest in collecting creatures inspired him to create Pokémon.

As a teenager, Tajiri played and designed video games. He taught himself how to program, or create instructions for games. He took apart video game devices to learn how they worked.

One day, he saw two players with Game Boys connected by a cable. He imagined insects crawling back and forth between the Game Boys. The idea for Pokémon was born.

By 2017, there were more than eight hundred different Pokémon. How many can you catch?

Traveling the World

Video game players in Japan loved Pokémon. The games were so successful that Nintendo released new versions of them. The new games had improved graphics and sound and introduced many new characters. The company brought the games to players around the world. *Pokémon Red* and *Pokémon Blue* came to the United States in 1998. Seven generations of Pokémon games, TV shows, and more were developed from 1996 to 2017. Each generation introduced new Pokémon and battle moves.

The games inspired a card game. In *Pokémon Trading Card Game*, players collect cards they use to battle other players. When a player knocks out an opponent's card, she picks up a prize card. The first player to pick up all six of her prize cards wins the match.

Pokémon Trading Card Game began in 1996. It originally had 102 cards with some of the Pokémon from the video games. The game grew until there were thousands of different Pokémon cards.

Players compete in *Pokémon Trading Card Game* tournaments around the world.

Chapter 2

CATCH YOUR POKÉMON!

Your Pokémon adventure starts when you enter the game's special world. Each Pokémon game takes place in a different region of the Pokémon world. As a trainer, you explore that region.

At the start of a Pokémon video game, a Professor appears. The Professor has studied the Pokémon of the region and lets you choose one of three Pokémon to get started. Then you look for wild Pokémon—creatures that have not been caught by a trainer. You throw Poké Balls to catch them.

Pokémon games are played on different devices such as phones, game consoles, and more.

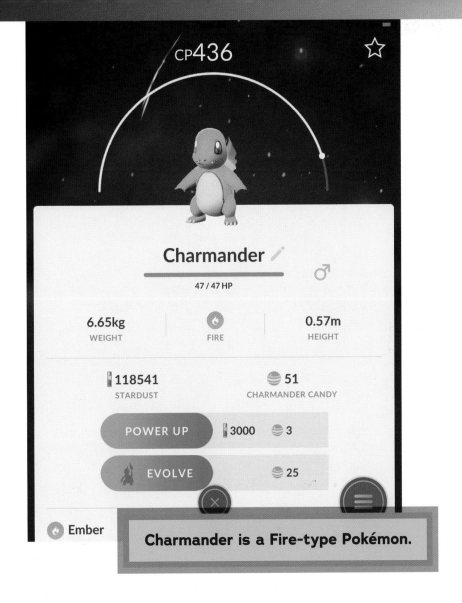

Charmander is a Fire-type Pokémon.

There are eighteen different types of Pokémon. Their type lets you know how they will perform in a battle. Fire-type Pokémon are strong against Grass-type Pokémon. That's easy to remember because fire burns grass. Fire types are weak against Water types. Water puts out fire. Some Pokémon have more than one type.

You learn your Pokémon's strengths and weaknesses as you journey. When you catch a Pokémon, its information is recorded in your Pokédex. To fill your Pokédex, you need to catch every Pokémon.

POKÉDEX
CAUGHT: 131 SEEN: 189

A Pokédex stores pictures and facts about each Pokémon you catch.

Meet Ken Sugimori

How did Satoshi Tajiri find someone to draw Pokémon? His friend Ken Sugimori illustrated a gaming magazine called *Game Freak*. Tajiri edited the magazine. He asked Sugimori to illustrate Pokémon.

Sugimori designed and drew all the original Pokémon. He makes illustrated trading cards and movies too. For modern games, Sugimori oversees many artists who work to create new Pokémon.

This trading card features Charmeleon, one of the earliest Pokémon.

Gengar ♀Lv.50

Blastoise Lv.46
134/134

Each trainer sends out one Pokémon to begin a battle.

Ready to Battle!

You'll meet other trainers on your journey. These trainers will challenge you to battles. You choose a team of up to six Pokémon to use in battle. It's important to choose Pokémon that have different strengths and weaknesses to form a balanced team.

When a battle begins, the trainers take turns selecting moves such as attacks. Some moves weaken the opposing Pokémon. Other moves may heal your Pokémon or make them stronger. Each Pokémon has a certain number of hit points. When a Pokémon loses all of its hit points, it faints and is defeated. The trainer with Pokémon left standing wins the battle.

Just as people get stronger and learn new skills as they grow, so do Pokémon! If a Pokémon defeats an opponent without fainting, it gets experience points. It levels up after a certain number of points.

Pokémon change into new, more powerful forms when they grow. They also evolve through trading and by using special items that trainers find on their journeys.

When a Pokémon's level increases, it gains new battle moves.

Your goal is to become the strongest trainer in the region. To do this, you visit Pokémon Gyms. A Gym is a place to train Pokémon and make them stronger. There you challenge the Gym Leader. If you defeat a Gym Leader's team of Pokémon, you earn a badge.

Once you earn eight badges, you're ready to take on the Pokémon League. The League is made up of the top trainers in the game's region. If you beat the League, you become the new region champion!

Chapter 3

FROM COMICS TO COSPLAY

You don't have to play video games to love Pokémon. Pokémon comics, cartoons, and movies have millions of fans. Stores sell Pokémon costumes and toys called Poké Plush. You can wear clothing from hats to socks that are decorated with your favorite Pokémon.

Fans dress up as Charizard (*left*) and Pikachu (*right*).

THE POKÉMON ADVENTURES SERIES IS ONE OF THE MOST POPULAR POKÉMON MANGA.

Manga are Japanese comics and graphic novels for children and adults. Pokémon manga take place in the Pokémon world. But the characters have different adventures than they do in the games. They explore new regions, fight evil, and conquer Pokémon Gyms.

Pokémon characters also star in anime—animated Japanese television shows and movies. Fans in countries around the world watch Pokémon anime.

There are more than nine hundred anime TV series and twenty movies. Most feature Ash Ketchum. Ash is a trainer from Pallet Town, a small town in the Pokémon world. The anime follow his journey to become a Pokémon Master. Ash battles different Gym Leaders and earns badges.

Ash Ketchum and Pikachu (*left*) appear in the 2001 movie *Pokémon 4Ever*.

Meet an Animator

How do Pokémon characters come to life on-screen? That's an animator's job. An animator draws many images of characters. The characters appear to move when the images are quickly shown one after another.

Some animators draw on paper. Others use computers for their creations. Animators learn special computer programs. The programs help them create characters, scenes, and backgrounds.

PokéFans!

Some fans like to dress up as Pokémon characters. They go to cosplay conventions. Cosplay is dressing and acting as a fictional character. PokéCon is a convention in Minneapolis that is just for Pokémon fans. People dress like trainers and Pokémon and compete in Pokémon games.

Attending Pokémon conventions is a great way for fans to meet people who share their interests.

013 WEEDLE

SEEN: 80   CAUGHT: 59

WEIGHT: 3.2 kg   HEIGHT: 0.3 m   TYPE: BUG / POISON

HAIRY BUG POKÉMON

Weedle has an extremely acute sense of smell. It is capable of distinguishing its favorite kinds of leaves from those it dislikes just by sniffing with its big red proboscis (nose).

EVOLUTION

A type of wasp was named after a Pokémon called a Weedle.

Many television shows and movies refer to Pokémon. On *The Simpsons*, Homer plays *Pokémon GO* while Lisa and Bart try to get his attention at the zoo. In the movie *Paper Towns*, three friends sing about catching Pokémon.

Even some scientists are Pokémon fans. Japanese scientists named a protein pikachurin. The protein has lightning-fast moves and electric powers like Pikachu! A type of wasp is named after a Pokémon called Weedle. The wasp has a spine in the middle of its head similar to a Weedle.

Chapter 4

POKÉMON ON THE GO!

In July 2016, a new Pokémon craze started. People around the world began playing *Pokémon GO* on their phones.

As a *Pokémon GO* player, you use a phone camera to view the world around you. Pokémon appear on the screen and look as if they're in the real world. As you explore your town, you can find more and more wild Pokémon.

As many as one hundred million people play *Pokémon GO* each month.

When you start playing *Pokémon GO*, a map appears on the phone screen. It shows nearby streets and paths. Suddenly a picture of a Magikarp pops up on-screen. You click on the picture, and the phone shows your surroundings. The Pokémon is in front of a lake! You toss a Poké Ball and catch the Magikarp.

Water-type Pokémon such as Magikarp are found near lakes and beaches.

The map also helps you find PokéStops and Gyms. PokéStops are places to gather Poké Balls and other items. You might find Pokémon Eggs to hatch in your Incubator. Maybe you'll collect healing items. Look for PokéStops and Gyms at parks, libraries, and other public places.

POKÉMON EGGS HATCH INTO NEW POKÉMON AFTER YOU WALK AT LEAST 1.2 MILES (2 KM).

Meet a Game Developer

Would you like to make video games? That's what a game developer does. Some developers create a game's stories and characters. They write programs that tell a machine such as a Game Boy how to run the game. Developers might work on small parts of a game, or they might design an entire game.

At the Gym!

In *Pokémon GO*, trainers gain experience and level up by catching and hatching Pokémon, winning battles, and completing other tasks. When you reach level 5, you're ready to join a team. There are three *Pokémon GO* teams: Red, Blue, and Yellow.

Teams battle to control Gyms. You help your team build a stronger Gym by placing Pokémon inside. Then the Gym's Prestige, or ranking, goes up. If another team controls a Gym, you can attack it. You try to defeat its Pokémon and lower the Gym's Prestige to zero. Then you control the Gym and can leave a Pokémon behind to protect it.

The original version of *Pokémon GO* didn't let players swap Pokémon. But Niantic, the company that makes *Pokémon GO*, plans to introduce trading. They may also allow players to battle one another. Then friends will be able to see who is the champion trainer!

New Pokémon will continue to appear on game consoles, mobile phones, and cards. And Pokémon fans will try to catch them all!

Pokémon GO players look for creatures at New York City's Central Park.

Bonus Points

- *Pokémon* is a combination of two Japanese words: *poketto* and *monsutā*. *Poketto* means "pocket," and *monsutā* means "monster." Pokémon are like small monsters that you collect and put in your pocket!

- Rhydon was the first Pokémon creature that Ken Sugimori created. It looks like a dinosaur. A statue of Rhydon appears in front of Gyms in many Pokémon games.

- Ekans and Arbok are two Pokémon that look like snakes. Can you guess how they got their names? Spelled backward, the names are *snake* and *kobra*!

- The Pokémon called Poliwag has a swirl on its belly. The intestines of tadpoles, or pollywogs, are swirl-shaped. Some pollywogs have see-through skin. Their spiral-shaped intestines look like Poliwag's belly!

Glossary

anime: a style of Japanese cartoon

cable: a wire with a protective covering

character: a person or creature that plays a part in a story

design: create something according to a plan

evolve: change

graphic: an image shown on a screen

illustrate: make drawings that are part of a story

incubator: a box that helps eggs hatch

manga: Japanese graphic novels or comic books

program: create instructions for a computer

protein: a type of chemical that is a part of all living things

Learn More about Video Games

Books

Kaplan, Arie. *The Epic Evolution of Video Games.* Minneapolis: Lerner Publications, 2014. Learn more about the history of video games in this fun book.

Polinsky, Paige V. *Pokémon Designer: Satoshi Tajiri.* Minneapolis: Abdo, 2017. This book brings Satoshi Tajiri's story to life.

Suen, Anastasia. *Alternate Reality Game Designer Jane McGonigal.* Minneapolis: Lerner Publications, 2014. Read all about the life of Jane McGonigal, one of the world's most respected video game designers.

Websites

How to Make a Toilet Roll Pikachu
https://www.youtube.com/watch?v=KI4X_TiXA_k
Watch this YouTube video to learn how to make Pikachu with a few simple materials.

Pokémon
http://www.pokemon.com/us
Visit the official Pokémon website for the latest news about games, shows, and much more.

Pokémon GO
http://www.pokemongo.com
The *Pokémon GO* website has all the info a fan of the game could want.

Index

Photo Acknowledgments

Image acknowledgments: Matthew Corley/Shutterstock.com, p. 4; kamui29/Shutterstock.com, p. 5; Yoshikazu Tsuno/AFP/Getty Images, p. 6; Kyodo News/Newscom, p. 7; Shogakukan/Tomy/Kobal/REX/Shutterstock, p. 8; Justin Sullivan/Getty Images, p. 9; iStock.com/anvmedia, p. 10; Images from Pokémon Go, pp. 11, 12, 22; Anthony Verde/The LIFE Images Collection/Getty Images, p. 13; Images from Pokémon Moon, pp. 14, 15, 16; Kepy/ZUMA Press Inc./Alamy Stock Photo, p. 17; Wachirawit Iemlerkchai/Alamy Stock Photo, p. 18; *Pokémon 4Ever*, 2002, © Miramax/Courtesy Everett Collection, p. 19; Warner Bros. Pictures/Getty Images, p. 20; mmckinneyphotography/Shutterstock.com, p. 21; iStock.com/ChrisHepburn, p. 23; Wachiwit/Shutterstock.com, p. 24; mama_mia/Shutterstock.com, p. 25; Pe3k/Shutterstock.com, p. 26; sarayu wanchai/Shutterstock.com, p. 27; Mark Kauzlarich/Reuters/Newscom, p. 28.

Cover: enchanted_fairy/Shutterstock.com.

Main body text set in Adrianna Regular 14/20.
Typeface provided by Chank.